A Note From Rick Renner

I am on a personal quest to see a "revival of the Bible" so people can establish their lives on a firm foundation that will stand strong and endure the test as end-time storm winds begin to intensify.

In order to experience a revival of the Bible in your personal life, it is important to take time each day to read, receive, and apply its truths to your life. James tells us that if we will continue in the perfect law of liberty — refusing to be forgetful hearers, but determined to be doers — we will be blessed in our ways. As you watch or listen to the programs in this series and work through this corresponding study guide, I trust you will search the Scriptures and allow the Holy Spirit to help you hear something new from God's Word that applies specifically to your life. I encourage you to be a doer of the Word He reveals to you. Whatever the cost, I assure you — it will be worth it.

> Thy words were found, and I did eat them;
> and thy word was unto me the joy and rejoicing of mine heart:
> for I am called by thy name, O Lord God of hosts.
> — Jeremiah 15:16

Your brother and friend in Jesus Christ,

Rick Renner

Unless otherwise indicated, all scripture quotations are taken from the *King James Version* of the Bible.

Scripture quotations marked (*AMPC*) are taken from the *Amplified® Bible.* Copyright © 1954, 1958, 1962, 1964, 1965, 1987 by The Lockman Foundation. Used by permission. www.Lockman.org.

Scripture quotations marked (*MSG*) are taken from *The Message,* copyright © 1993, 2002, 2018 by Eugene H. Peterson. Used by permission of NavPress. All rights reserved. Represented by Tyndale House Publishers, Inc.

Scripture quotations marked (*TLB*) are taken from *The Living Bible* copyright © 1971. Used by permission of Tyndale House Publishers, Inc., Carol Stream, Illinois 60188. All rights reserved.

Windows Into Divine Revelation

Copyright © 2022 by Rick Renner
1814 W. Tacoma St.
Broken Arrow, OK 74012-1406

Published by Rick Renner Ministries
www.renner.org

ISBN 13: 978-1-6675-0306-6

eBook ISBN 13: 978-1-6675-0307-3

All rights reserved. No portion of this book may be reproduced or transmitted in any form or by any means — electronic, mechanical, photocopy, recording, scanning, or other — except for brief quotations in critical reviews or articles, without the prior written permission of the Publisher.

How To Use This Study Guide

This five-lesson study guide corresponds to *"Windows Into Divine Revelation" With Rick Renner* (Renner TV). Each lesson in this study guide covers a topic that is addressed during the program series, with questions and references supplied to draw you deeper into your own private study of the Scriptures on this subject.

To derive the most benefit from this study guide, consider the following:

First, watch or listen to the program prior to working through the corresponding lesson in this guide. (Programs can also be viewed at **renner.org** by clicking on the Media/Archives links or on our Renner Ministries YouTube channel.)

Second, take the time to look up the scriptures included in each lesson. Prayerfully consider their application to your own life.

Third, use a journal or notebook to make note of your answers to each lesson's Study Questions and Practical Application challenges.

Fourth, invest specific time in prayer and in the Word of God to consult with the Holy Spirit. Write down the scriptures or insights He reveals to you.

Finally, take action! Whatever the Lord tells you to do according to His Word, do it.

For added insights on this subject, it is recommended that you obtain Rick Renner's books *Sparkling Gems From the Greek, Volumes 1* **and** *2*. You may also select from Rick's other available resources by placing your order at **renner.org** or by calling 1-800-742-5593.

LESSON 1

TOPIC
The Source of Divine Revelation

SCRIPTURES
1. **1 Corinthians 2:9,10,12** — But as it is written, Eye hath not seen, nor ear heard, neither have entered into the heart of man, the things which God hath prepared for them that love him. But God hath revealed them unto us by his Spirit: for the Spirit searcheth all things, yea, the deep things of God.... Now we have received, not the spirit of the world, but the spirit which is of God; that we might know the things that are freely given to us of God.

GREEK WORDS
1. "eye" — ὀφθαλμὸς (*ophthalmos*): the eye; a single eye
2. "not" — οὐκ (*ouk*): the most emphatic form of no or not
3. "seen" — ὁράω (*horao*): to behold, delightfully view, experience, fully view, look, perceive, see, or view
4. "nor" — καί (*kai*): and, or additionally
5. "ear" — οὖς (*ous*): ear; a single ear; no ear has heard or perceived
6. "heard" — ἀκούω (*akouo*): to hear; carries the idea of comprehension
7. "neither" — καί (*kai*): and, or additionally
8. "entered' — ἀναβαίνω (*anabaino*): to ascend, to rise, to move upward, or to transition upward
9. "the things" — ὅσα (*hosa*): what; how great; how much; speaking of the vast extent of things
10. "prepared" — ἕτοιμος (*hetoimos*): a word that was used to depict a state of preparedness; inherent in the word is the action of one who has done his part to be prepared for a specific event; used in an athletic sense to depict runners who had prepared in advance for a race; used in a military sense to portray soldiers who had their shoes tied on very tightly and, hence, had a firm footing; as such, these soldiers were prepared for action and were ready at any moment to be called upon for duty

11. "but" — γάρ (*gar*): but indeed
12. "revealed" — ἀποκαλύπτω (*apokalupto*): a compound of the preposition ἀπό (*apo*) and καλύπτω (*kalupto*); the preposition ἀπό (*apo*) means away, as to remove something, and the word καλύπτω (*kalupto*) means to conceal, as to hide or to obstruct; when compounded, it refers to something that has been veiled or hidden but then becomes clear and visible to the mind or eye; a sudden revealing; an unveiling or, thus, to uncover; because the veil has been removed, what is behind the veil is no longer concealed or hidden from view
13. "unto us" — ἡμῖν (*hemin*): to us; directly to us
14. "by" — διά (*dia*): by or through; indicates agency and instrumentality; carries the idea of going back and forth in order to go all the way through, as one who crosses to the other side; here, we find the never-give-up work of the Spirit to reveal what God wants to show us
15. "His Spirit" — τοῦ Πνεύματος (*tou Pneumatos*): by His Spirit, meaning the Holy Spirit
16. "for" — γάρ (*gar*): for; indeed
17. "searcheth" — ἐρευνάω (*ereunao*): to investigate, to examine, or to sift; pictures one who goes through stacks of material looking for something; one who carefully investigates, examines, and sifts through the materials as he searches for what he needs
18. "all things" — πάντα (*panta*): all things; down to the precise details, leaving nothing out
19. "yea" — καί (*kai*): even; indeed; moreover
20. "deep things" — τὰ βάθη (*ta bathe*): from the word βάθος (*bathos*), meaning the deepest parts of the sea; can denote deep thoughts, deep spiritual truths, or deeply laid plans; the use of τὰ (*ta*) amplifies the vast number of God's plans
21. "now" — δέ (*de*): intended to make an exclamatory, dramatic point; but now
22. "but" — ἀλλά (*alla*): but instead
23. "that" — ἵνα (*hina*): points to an express purpose
24. "know" — οἶδα (*oida*): to comprehend, perceive, see, or understand
25. "the things" — τὰ (*ta*): the many things; the extent of vast, great things
26. "freely given" — χάρις (*charis*): here, the tense means graced
27. "to us" — ἡμῖν (*hemin*): to us; directly to us

28. "of" God — ὑπό (*hupo*): by, or under; implying this comes by or from God, and comes to those who are under his Lordship

SYNOPSIS

The five lessons in this study, ***Windows Into Divine Revelation***, will focus on the following topics:

- **The Source of Divine Revelation**
- **The Role of Tongues in Receiving Divine Revelation**
- **A Prayer for Divine Revelation, Part 1**
- **A Prayer for Divine Revelation, Part 2**
- **Paul's Prayer for Divine Comprehension**

The emphasis of this lesson:
There are many things in our lives vying for our attention — some good and some bad. Either way, they can distract us from what's eternal and of priceless value. God wants to pull back the curtain to give you divine revelation into the realm of the spirit and give you eyes to see things you've never seen before.

In First Corinthians 2:9, it says, "But as it is written, Eye hath not seen, nor ear heard, neither have entered into the heart of man, the things which God hath prepared for them that love him." Some have misinterpreted this verse to mean that there is no way for us to really see and understand certain things, such as knowing what to do or say in a given situation or comprehending what the future holds. But thankfully this perception is incorrect! There's so much that we *can* see and know about God and His will for us.

'Eye Hath Not Seen, Nor Ear Heard'

Writing under the anointing of the Holy Spirit, the apostle Paul said, "Eye hath not seen, nor ear heard, neither have entered into the heart of man, the things which God hath prepared for them that love him" (1 Corinthians 2:9). Let's take time to unpack this verse and grasp more fully what God is saying to us.

First, notice the word "eye." It is the Greek word *ophthalmos*, and it denotes *the eye or a single eye*. It is where we get the word *ophthalmology*, describing *the study of the eyes*. The word "not" is the Greek word *ouk*, the most emphatic form of no or not, and the word "seen" is the Greek word *horao*, which means *to behold, to delightfully view, to experience, to fully view, to look, to perceive, see,* or *view*. When we take all these meanings together, this portion of the verse could be translated:

> **Not even one single eye has seen, perceived, fully viewed, or experienced....**

Paul then added, "...Nor ear heard..." (1 Corinthians 2:9). In Greek, the word "nor" is *kai*, which means *and* or *additionally*. The word "ear" is the Greek word *ous*, which is the term for the *ear*, and here specifically describes *a single ear*. The word "heard" in Greek is *akouo*, which means *to hear* and carries the idea of *comprehension*. It is where we get the word *acoustics*. Putting all these meanings together, the verse could be translated:

> **Not even one single eye has seen, perceived, fully viewed, or experienced, and not even one single ear has ever had the ability to hear, comprehend, or understand....**

'Neither Have Entered Into the Heart of Man'

The next phrase is "...neither have entered into the heart of man..." (1 Corinthians 2:9). The word "neither" is the word *kai*, the same word translated as "nor" just a few words before it. Again, it means *and* or *additionally*, and the Greek word for "entered" is *anabaino*, which means *to ascend, to rise, to move upward,* or *to transition upward*.

Sometimes this word is translated as "imagine," which is why the verse says, "neither have entered into the heart of man." The indication is that no man has ever begun to *imagine* or *conceive* the things that God has prepared for those who love Him.

'The Things Which God Hath Prepared'

In Greek, "the things" is a translation of the word *hosa*, which means *what, how great,* or *how much*. It speaks of *the vast extent of things* that God has prepared for those who love Him.

Up to this point, this verse is clearly telling us that there was a time when not a single eye had seen or perceived and not a single ear had the ability to hear or understand, and neither had it risen in the heart of man or had a man ever imagined the vast extent of things God had prepared for him.

This brings us to the word "prepared" — the Greek word *hetoimos*, which is a word that was used to depict *a state of preparedness*. Inherent in this word is the action of one who has done his part to be prepared for a specific event. This word was used in an athletic sense to depict runners who had prepared in advance for a race, and in a military sense, it was used to portray soldiers who had their shoes tied on very tightly and, hence, had a firm footing. As such, these soldiers were prepared for action and were ready at any moment to be called upon for duty.

So, according to First Corinthians 2:9, God has not just prepared things for you, but the vast extent of things He's prepared are ready to move in your direction. They are in a state of preparedness, ready to move at any moment they're called upon for duty, to come and begin working in your life. And this is for anyone who loves Him. If your heart is fixed on Jesus, He has marvelous things prepared for you!

God Reveals What Has Been Hidden

Now between verses 9 and 10 something shifts. What was once hidden has now been brought out into full view. The Bible says, "But God hath revealed them unto us by his Spirit: for the Spirit searcheth all things, yea, the deep things of God" (1 Corinthians 2:10).

Notice the first word "but." It is the Greek word *gar* and would better be translated *but indeed*. Its use here is the equivalent of the apostle Paul raising his voice and emphatically saying, "*But indeed*, God hath revealed them unto us by His Spirit…." Revealed what things? God revealed the vast extent of things He has prepared and are waiting to appear and move into action.

The word "revealed" is a form of the Greek word *apokalupto*, which is a compound of the preposition *apo* and the word *kalupto*. *Apo* means *away*, as to remove something, and the word *kalupto* means *to conceal*, as *to hide* or *to obstruct*. When compounded, the new word *apokalupto* refers to *something that has been veiled or hidden but then becomes clear and visible to the mind or eye*. It is *a sudden revealing* or *an unveiling*. Thus, because the veil has been removed, what was behind it is no longer concealed or hidden from view.

This scripture says what was once hidden or concealed from our view or our understanding has suddenly come into full view "unto us." The Greek word for "unto us" is *hemin*, and it means *to us* or *directly to us*. Part of the ministry of the Holy Spirit is to remove the veil of obscurity over the things about God, ourselves, and our future so that we can see and comprehend them and know what to do.

It's Through the Agency of His Spirit

What is the source of this emphatic, sudden unveiling? Paul said, "But God hath revealed them unto us *by his Spirit...*" (1 Corinthians 2:10). The word "by" here is important. It is the little Greek word *dia*, which means *by* or *through*. Hence, this revealing of what was once hidden comes *by* or *through* the Holy Spirit.

This word *dia* also indicates *agency and instrumentality*, which means we could translate this part of the verse, "But God has revealed them unto us *through the agency of* the Holy Spirit..." or "*through the instrumentality of* the Holy Spirit...." Moreover, the word *dia* — translated here as "by" — also carries the idea of going back and forth in order to go all the way through, as one who crosses to the other side. Here, we find a picture of the never-give-up work of the Spirit to reveal what God wants to show us. He'll go back and forth with us, never giving up, until finally the curtain is completely pulled back and we can clearly see all we need to see and understand.

Again, this divine unveiling is done by the agency or instrumentality of "His Spirit." This phrase is a translation of the Greek words *tou Pneumatos*, and it means *by His Spirit*. In Greek, the word *Pneumatos* — translated as "Spirit" — is capitalized, which makes it absolutely clear that it is *the Holy Spirit* being talked about here.

The Spirit 'Searcheth All Things'

First Corinthians 2:10 goes on to say, "...For the Spirit searcheth all things, yea, the deep things of God." Once more we see the word "for" — the Greek word *gar* — meaning *for* or *indeed*. It indicates that Paul was making an emphatic statement. In this case, he was exclaiming that the Holy Spirit "searcheth all things." The word "searcheth" is the Greek word *ereunao*, and it means *to investigate, to examine*, or *to sift*. It pictures *one who goes through stacks and stacks of material looking for something or one who carefully investigates, examines, and sifts through the materials as he searches for what he needs.*

Here, the Holy Spirit is carefully examining and sifting through "all things." In Greek, this is the word *panta*, which describes *all things*. It is a thorough investigation down to the precise details, leaving nothing out. This means when the Holy Spirit comes to reveal the will of God to you, He first does His investigative work to locate exactly what the will of God is for your life, which includes vital answers regarding whom you should marry, what job you should take, and where you should invest and spend your money. Whatever is concerning you concerns the Holy Spirit, moving Him to search for the exact answer, all things down to the most minute detail.

Paul said, "…Yea, the deep things of God" (1 Corinthians 2:10). The word "yea" is a translation of the Greek word *kai*, which means *even*, *indeed*, or *moreover*. "Deep things" in Greek is *ta bathe* and is from the word *bathos*, which describes *the deepest parts of the sea*. It can denote *deep thoughts, deep spiritual truths*, or *deeply laid plans*. The use of the word *ta* here amplifies the vast number of God's plans for our life. This lets us know that when the Holy Spirit moves into His investigative mode, He doesn't just search out things on the surface; He dives deep to find the answers we need.

It Is God's Spirit That Has Graced Us With Great Things

To make sure we understand the source of divine revelation in our lives, Paul wrote, "Now we have received, not the spirit of the world, but the spirit which is of God; that we might know the things that are freely given to us of God" (1 Corinthians 2:12). The word "now" is the Greek word *de*, which is intended to make *an exclamatory, dramatic point*. It's like Paul was loudly exclaiming, "But now, we have not received the spirit of this world!"

The conjunction "but" is the Greek word *alla*, which means *but instead* or *on the other hand*. Paul said, "We haven't received the spirit of this world, *but instead*, we have received the Spirit of God that we might know the things that are freely given to us of God." The word "that" is the Greek word *hina*, and it points to *an express purpose* — that purpose is *that we might know the things that are freely given to us of God*.

In this verse, the word "know" is the Greek word *oida*, which means *to comprehend, perceive, see, or understand*. The Spirit of God helps us *perceive* and *understand* "the things" — the Greek word *ta*, meaning *the many things* or *the extent of vast, great things*. God wants us to fully comprehend all the things He's "freely given to us." The phrase "freely given" is a form of the Greek word *charis*, which is the word for *grace*. Here, the tense means *graced*, which lets us know that we don't earn what God gives and we don't deserve what God gives "to us."

Once more, the Greek word *hemin* is used, and here it's translated "to us," which means *directly to us*. Every blessed thing that we are graced with is "of" God. The word "of" is the Greek word *hupo*, and it means *by* or *under*, implying this comes *by* or *from* God and comes to those who are *under* His Lordship.

Friend, God wants to give you revelation and show you the vast catalog of things He has prepared for you. He wants to pull back the curtain and show you things you've never seen. Surrender to His lordship, and His Spirit — the source of all divine revelation — will begin revealing things to you that are simply astounding!

STUDY QUESTIONS

Study to shew thyself approved unto God, a workman that needeth not to be ashamed, rightly dividing the word of truth.
— 2 Timothy 2:15

1. Joseph and Daniel are two people in the Old Testament whom the Holy Spirit empowered through divine revelation. Take some time to reflect on each man's story in Genesis 41:14-45 and Daniel 2. With what divine revelations did the Spirit grace Joseph and Daniel, and how did they respond to having such knowledge? How were their lives changed as a result? What do their examples speak to you personally?
2. First Corinthians 2:9 tells us that God has many great things prepared for those who love Him. Take a few moments to check out a small sampling of the blessings God has ready and waiting to show up in your life as you live in relationship with Him and obey Him:

- **Deuteronomy 28:1-14**
- **Psalm 5:12; 23:6**

- James 1:17 and Psalm 34:9,10; 84:11
- Proverbs 16:7

PRACTICAL APPLICATION

> But be ye doers of the word, and not hearers only, deceiving your own selves.
> — James 1:22

1. Right here and now, God has so much good waiting for you, and you've only just begun to see most of it! How does it encourage you to know that He has meticulously prepared good things for you that could arrive on the scene at any moment?
2. Is it hard for you to perceive the good things God has waiting in the wings? Pray and ask the Holy Spirit to help you begin to see into the realm of the spirit and perceive the good that is all around you. (*Consider* the story in Second Kings 6:15-17.)
3. The fact that the Holy Spirit "searches all things" means every answer you'll ever need to know what to do in any situation is available to you. What is one life question that God has already answered? What is a question you need Him to answer *right now*? Where do you most need His direction? Pray and make your need known to Him, trusting Him to answer.

LESSON 2

TOPIC
The Role of Tongues in Receiving Divine Revelation

SCRIPTURES

1. **1 Corinthians 2:9,10,12** — But as it is written, Eye hath not seen, nor ear heard, neither have entered into the heart of man, the things which God hath prepared for them that love him. But God hath revealed them unto us by his Spirit: for the Spirit searcheth all things,

yea, the deep things of God.... Now we have received, not the spirit of the world, but the spirit which is of God; that we might know the things that are freely given to us of God.

2. **1 Corinthians 2:14** — But the natural man receiveth not the things of the Spirit of God: for they are foolishness unto him: neither can he know them, because they are spiritually discerned.
3. **1 Corinthians 14:2** — For he that speaketh in an unknown tongue speaketh not unto men, but unto God: for no man understandeth him; howbeit in the spirit he speaketh mysteries.
4. **1 Corinthians 14:4** — He that speaketh in an unknown tongue edifieth himself....

GREEK WORDS

1. "but" — γάρ (*gar*): but indeed
2. "revealed" — ἀποκαλύπτω (*apokalupto*): a compound of the preposition ἀπό (*apo*) and καλύπτω (*kalupto*); the preposition ἀπό (*apo*) means away, as to remove something, and the word καλύπτω (*kalupto*) means to conceal, as to hide or to obstruct; when compounded, it refers to something that has been veiled or hidden but then becomes clear and visible to the mind or eye; a sudden revealing; an unveiling or, thus, to uncover; because the veil has been removed, what is behind the veil is no longer concealed or hidden from view
3. "unto us" — ἡμῖν (*hemin*): to us; directly to us
4. "by" — διά (*dia*): by or through; indicates agency and instrumentality; carries the idea of going back and forth in order to go all the way through, as one who crosses to the other side; here, we find the never-give-up work of the Spirit to reveal what God wants to show us
5. "His Spirit" — τοῦ Πνεύματος (*tou Pneumatos*): by His Spirit, meaning the Holy Spirit
6. "for" — γάρ (*gar*): for; indeed
7. "searcheth" — ἐρευνάω (*ereunao*): to investigate, to examine, or to sift; pictures one who goes through stacks of material looking for something; one who carefully investigates, examines, and sifts through the materials as he searches for what he needs
8. "all things" — πάντα (*panta*): all things; down to the precise details, leaving nothing out
9. "yea" — καί (*kai*): even; indeed; moreover

10. "deep things" — τὰ βάθη (*ta bathe*): from the word βάθος (*bathos*), meaning the deepest parts of the sea; can denote deep thoughts, deep spiritual truths, or deeply laid plans; the use of τὰ (*ta*) amplifies the vast number of God's plans
11. "now" — δέ (*de*): intended to make an exclamatory, dramatic point; but now
12. "but" — ἀλλά (*alla*): but instead
13. "that" — ἵνα (*hina*): points to an express purpose
14. "know" — οἶδα (*oida*): to comprehend, perceive, see, or understand
15. "the things" — τὰ (*ta*): the many things; the extent of vast, great things
16. "freely given" — χάρις (*charis*): here, the tense means graced
17. "to us" — ἡμῖν (*hemin*): to us; directly to us
18. "by" God — ὑπό (*hupo*): by, or under; implying this comes by or from God, and comes to those who are under his Lordship
19. "natural man" — Ψυχικός ἄνθρωπος (*psuchikos anthropos*): the word ψυχικός (*psuchikos*) means soulish, and ἄνθρωπος (*anthropos*) means a person; depicts a soulish person or a person who merely operates out of his soul
20. "receiveth not" — οὐ δέχεται (*ou dechetai*): the word οὐ (*ou*) is a negative, and δέχεται (*dechetai*), from δέχομαι (*dechomai*), means to gladly and readily welcome; thus, to embrace; as a phrase, does not embrace, gladly receive, or readily welcome
21. "the things" — τὰ (*ta*): the many things; pictures the vast, great things
22. "foolishness" — μωρία (*moria*): from μωρός (*moros*), where we get the word moron; but μωρία (*moria*) means absurd, foolish, or stupid
23. "to him" — αὐτῷ (*auto*): to the man who is soulish or soul-dominated
24. "neither can" — οὐ δύναται (*ou dunatai*): does not have the ability or power; refers to the inability of a soulish person to perceive spiritual things
25. "know" — γινώσκω (*ginosko*): to know, perceive, realize, or recognize
26. "because" — ὅτι (*hoti*): explicitly because
27. "spiritually discerned" — πνευματικῶς ἀνακρίνεται (*pneumatikos anakrinetai*): the word πνευματικῶς (*pneumatikos*) means spiritually, in a spiritual way, or from a spiritual point of view; the word ἀνακρίνεται (*anakrinetai*), from ἀνακρίνω (*anakrino*), pictures analyzing, examining, investigating, judging, or sifting; as a phrase,

it means spiritually comprehended, spiritually judged, or spiritually understood

28. "for" — γάρ (*gar*): for; indeed
29. "speaketh" — λαλέω (*laleo*): to chatter or to converse, as to converse in a language or to carry on a conversation; hence, he who chatters, converses, or carries on a conversation
30. "unknown tongue" — γλῶσσα (*glossa*): a tongue, language, or flowing speech; here, a language not naturally known
31. "not" — οὐκ (*ouk*): the most emphatic form of no or not
32. "unto men" — ἀνθρώποις (*anthropois*): to humans or to people
33. "but unto God" — ἀλλὰ Θεῷ (*alla Theo*): but instead; but on the other hand; but conversely; to God; when one prays in the Spirit, it is directed to God
34. "howbeit" — δέ (*de*): intended to make a dramatic point
35. "in the spirit" — πνεύματι (*pneumati*): in spirit; refers to the type of language being spoken; not a naturally learned language, but a spiritual language
36. "he speaketh" — λαλέω (*laleo*): to chatter or to converse, as to converse in a language or to carry on a conversation; hence, he who chatters, converses, or carries on a conversation
37. "mysteries" — μυστήριον (*musterion*): things hidden; secrets; mysteries; something which can only be comprehended, known, or seen by revelation
38. "edifieth" — οἰκοδομή (*oikodome*): an architectural term meaning to enlarge or amplify a house; it depicts the careful following of an architectural plan to enlarge, increase, or amplify; to edify; to improve; to leave in an improved condition

SYNOPSIS

The typical houses of the upper class in Seventeenth Century Russia were simply magnificent. During that era, their homes were constructed of quarried stone and ornate masonry, and around their windows were beautifully carved stone decorations. Those less fortunate couldn't afford homes made of stone and masonry, so they were mostly made of wood. Likewise, the decorations around their windows were made of very colorful wooden latticework.

In both cases, the reasoning behind having decorative window surroundings was to keep people from looking through the window into the house. Thus, the ornamentation was meant to distract the attention of onlookers and protect the homeowners' privacy.

In a spiritual sense, we have a great deal of "latticework" in our lives that is distracting us and obstructing our view of what is most important. God wants to give us divine revelation into the windows of Heaven and show us deep things we have never seen before, and the gift of tongues plays a vital role in receiving His revelation.

The emphasis of this lesson:

When we pray in the spiritual language of tongues, the Holy Spirit pulls back the curtain, enabling us to see and understand things about ourselves, about God, and about life that we could never have seen on our own.

A Review of Lesson 1

From Concealed to Revealed. Before Jesus came and gave His life for our redemption, our spiritual vision and understanding were extremely limited. In fact, the apostle Paul said, "…Eye hath not seen, nor ear heard, neither have entered into the heart of man, the things which God hath prepared for them that love him" (1 Corinthians 2:9). Although this era of ignorance was once a reality, that is no longer the case. God has made a way for us to be able to see more and more of what He has for us.

Paul said, "…God hath revealed them unto us by his Spirit: for the Spirit searcheth all things, yea, the deep things of God" (1 Corinthians 2:10). We saw in Lesson 1 that the word "revealed" is a translation of the Greek word *apokalupto*, which is a compound of the words *apo* and *kalupto*. The preposition *apo* means *away*, as *to remove something*, and the word *kalupto* means *to conceal*, as *to hide or to obstruct*. When compounded to form the word *apokalupto*, it describes *something that has been veiled or hidden but then becomes clear and visible to the mind or eye*. It is *a sudden revealing or an unveiling*. What was once behind the veil is no longer concealed or hidden from view.

It's by the Spirit. This eye-opening reveal that God desires to regularly bring about in your life is a work of the Holy Spirit. First Corinthians 2:10 declares, "…God hath revealed them unto us *by his Spirit*.…" The phrase "unto us" is *hemin* in Greek, and it means *directly to us*. The ministry of the Holy Spirit includes removing the veil of obscurity and revealing truth directly to us. Again, enlightenment is "by His Spirit," and the word "by" is the Greek word *dia*, which means *by* or *through*. Hence, the answers we need come to us *by* or *through* the Holy Spirit.

The word *dia* also indicates *agency and instrumentality*, which means we could translate this part of the verse, "But God has revealed them unto us *through the agency of* the Spirit…" or "*through the instrumentality of* the Spirit…." Additionally, this word *dia* — translated here as "by" — also carries the idea of going back and forth in order to convince someone of something and get them all the way through to the other side. This is a picture of the never-give-up work of the Spirit to reveal what God wants to show us. He'll go back and forth with us until finally the curtain is completely pulled back and we can clearly see all we need to see and understand.

The Spirit Searches All Things. First Corinthians 2:10 says, "…For the Spirit searcheth all things, yea, the deep things of God." The word "for" here is the Greek word *gar* — meaning *for* or *indeed*. Paul's use of this word signifies that he was speaking emphatically about the revelatory work of the Holy Spirit. It's as if he was saying, "Indeed! The Spirit searches all things." We noted that the word "searcheth" is the Greek word *ereunao*, and it means *to investigate, to examine*, or *to sift*. It pictures *one who goes through stacks and stacks of material looking for something*. Here, it is the Holy Spirit who *carefully investigates, examines, and sifts through things* to discover and reveal to us God's plan and purpose.

This brings us to the words "all things," which in Greek is the word *panta*. The first part of the word — *pan* — means *all, nothing excluded*, and *ta* describes *things*. Hence, this is a thorough investigation down to the precise details with no stone left unturned. What is the Holy Spirit after? Paul said, "…Yea, the deep things of God" (1 Corinthians 2:10). The word "yea" is the Greek word *kai*, which means *even* or *indeed*. It's as if he was saying, "Even the deep things of God."

In Greek, the phrase "deep things" is *ta bathe*, from the word *bathos*, which describes *the deepest parts of the sea*. It can denote *deep thoughts, deep spiritual truths*, or *deeply laid plans*. The insertion of the word *ta* here amplifies the vast number of plans God has for our life — some of which are very deep. If you need help understanding God's will for your life, invite the

Holy Spirit to dive into the deep things of God and bring to the surface the answers you need.

God Has Graced Us With Many Wonderful Things. Paul wrote, "Now we have received, not the spirit of the world, but the spirit which is of God; that we might know the things that are freely given to us of God" (1 Corinthians 2:12). The word "now" here is the Greek word *de*, which is intended to make *an exclamatory, dramatic point*. It's the equivalent of Paul saying, "Now hear this! We have not received the spirit of this world, but the spirit which is of God!"

The word "but" is the Greek word *alla*, which means *but instead* or *on the other hand*. It marks the contrast between what we have and have not received. Paul said, "We haven't received the spirit of this world, *but instead*, we have received the Spirit of God that we might know the things that are freely given to us of God." The word "that" in Greek is *hina*, and it points to *an express purpose* — that purpose is *that we might know the things that are freely given to us of God*.

The Spirit of God helps us "know" — the Greek word *oida* — the things freely given to us of God. In other words, the Spirit enables us *to comprehend, perceive, and understand* "the things of God." In Greek, "the things" is the tiny word *ta*, and it describes t*he vast number of great things* God has "freely given" to us. The words "freely given" are a form of the Greek word *charis*, which literally means *graced* in this verse. There are numerous great things God has graced you with, but you can't discover them on your own. You can only experience them through the agency or instrumentality of the Spirit.

Note: these things are freely given "to us of God." The words "to us" are a translation of the Greek word *hemin*, which indicates *directly to us*. And the word "of" is the Greek word *hupo*, which means *by* or *under*, implying this comes *by* or *from* God and comes directly to us as we are living *under* the Lordship of Jesus Christ.

We Need To Be Spiritually Minded

Now, you may be wondering, *If the Holy Spirit wants to reveal great things to me, why am I not experiencing it?* The apostle Paul shed light on a major reason in First Corinthians 2:14 where he says, "But the natural man receiveth not the things of the Spirit of God: for they are foolishness unto him: neither can he know them, because they are spiritually discerned."

In this verse, the term "natural man" is a translation of the Greek words *psuchikos anthropos*. The word *psuchikos* means *soulish*, and *anthropos* means *a person*. Together, *psuchikos anthropos* depicts *a soulish person or a person who merely operates out of his soul*. In other words, this is a person who lives his life out of his mind or logic, or out of his emotions.

Anyone who functions out of his soul "…receiveth not the things of the Spirit of God…" (1 Corinthians 2:14). In Greek, "receiveth not" is *ou dechetai*. The word *ou* is a negative that negates or cancels; and *dechetai* is from the word *dechomai*, which means *to gladly and readily welcome or to embrace*. When compounded into the phrase *ou dechetai*, it means *does not embrace, does not gladly receive or readily welcome*. The soulish person *does not* embrace or gladly receive the things of God.

Once more we see the Greek word *ta* translated as "the things." It means *the many things* and pictures *the vast, great things* God has prepared for us. The person living on the lower level of the soul sees the things of God as "foolishness," which is the Greek word *moria*, taken from *moros*, which is where we get the word *moron*. Essentially, the word *moria* describes something *absurd, foolish*, or *stupid*. When the natural man hears and sees spiritual things, he turns his nose up. To him, it's just *stupid*. He doesn't understand it, and consequently, he doesn't like it. The words "to him" are a translation of the Greek word *auto*, which means *to the man who is soulish* or *soul-dominated*.

Spiritual Things Are Spiritually Discerned

In First Corinthians 2:14, Paul went on to say, "…Neither can he know them, because they are spiritually discerned." The words "neither can" are a translation of the Greek expression *ou dunatai*, which means *does not have the ability or power*. This refers to the *inability* of a soulish person to perceive spiritual things. The Bible says he is unable to "know" them. This word "know" is the Greek term *ginosko*, which means *to know, to perceive, to realize*, or *to recognize something*.

The natural, soulish man has no ability within himself to recognize and understand spiritual things "…because they are spiritually discerned" (1 Corinthians 2:14). The Greek word for "because" is *hoti*, meaning *explicitly because*, and the phrase "spiritually discerned" in Greek is *pneumatikos anakrinetai*. The first word *pneumatikos* means *spiritually, in a spiritual way*, or *from a spiritual point of view*. The word *anakrinetai* is from the word *anakrino*, and it pictures *analyzing, examining, investigating, judging*, or *sifting*. As a phrase, *pneumatikos anakrinetai* means *spiritually comprehended, spiritually judged*, or *spiritually understood*. Spiritual things are only understood and accurately perceived from a spiritual perspective.

So how can you see and understand what God has prepared for you? How can you peer through a window into the realm of the spirit so that you can accurately spiritually judge and spiritually comprehend the many wonderful things God has waiting in a state of preparedness for you? The answer is by speaking in the language of the spirit.

When We Speak in 'Tongues' We Converse With God, Not People

In First Corinthians 14:2, Paul gave us the key that unlocks the door to the realm of the spirit. He says, "For he that speaketh in an unknown tongue speaketh not unto men, but unto God: for no man understandeth him; howbeit in the spirit he speaketh mysteries."

Once more, the word "for" at the beginning of this verse is the Greek word *gar*, meaning *for* or *indeed*. It indicates that Paul was speaking *emphatically* and with *certainty*. The word "speaketh" is a form of the Greek term *laleo*, which means *to chatter* or *to converse*, as *to converse in a language* or *to carry on a conversation*. Hence, we could translate this part of the verse, *He who chatters in tongues, converses in tongues*, or *carries on a conversation in tongues*.

In Greek, the phrase "unknown tongue" is a translation of the word *glossa*, and it describes *a tongue, language*, or *flowing speech*. Here, it depicts *a language not naturally known*. Paul then inserted the word "speaketh" — the Greek word *laleo* — a second time. Thus, he is telling us, "Those who *chatter, converse, or carry on a conversation*, flowing in a language not naturally known, *chatters, converses, or carries on a conversation* not unto men, but unto God."

The word "not" here is *ouk* in Greek, which is *the most emphatic form of no or not*, and the phrase "unto men" is the Greek word *anthropois*, which means *to humans* or *to people*. The fact that Paul said, "Not (*ouk*) unto men, but unto God," tells us clearly that speaking in tongues is language directed toward God, not human beings. In fact, the phrase "but unto God" — *alla Theo* in Greek — means *but instead; but on the other hand; but conversely; to God*. When one prays in the Spirit, he or she is praying directly to God.

The Spirit Reveals Deep Mysteries to Us

Paul continued, "...For no man understandeth him; howbeit in the spirit he speaketh mysteries" (1 Corinthians 14:2). The word "howbeit" is the little Greek word *de*, which is intended to make a dramatic point. When a person chatters or converses in tongues, people don't understand it because he "speaketh" — again the Greek word *laleo*, meaning *chatters or speaks* — "mysteries."

This word "mysteries" in Greek is *musterion*, and it describes *things hidden*; *secrets*; or *mysteries*. It is *something which can only be comprehended, known, or seen by revelation*. So, First Corinthians 14:2 tells us that when we pray in tongues, the Holy Spirit goes to work, and He begins to dive deep inside us and pull up mysteries out of our spirit.

Friend, the day you were born again, the will of God for your life was placed inside you in the Person of the Holy Spirit. The Spirit of God has the mind of God, and He precisely knows God's will and purpose for your life.

When you begin to pray in the Spirit — chattering and conversing in tongues — you communicate with God in the Spirit on the deepest level possible. The Holy Spirit is then activated to go to work inside you, dredging your spirit to pull up the secret plans and hidden mysteries of God.

The Spirit then begins to reveal those mysteries to your mind. In those illuminating moments, it feels as though someone has suddenly pulled the cord on the curtains and they start to open. More and more, you begin to see through the window of divine revelation to the other side and can understand God's will for your life. Praying in tongues pulls back the curtains so you can see the revelation you so desperately need.

STUDY QUESTIONS

> Study to shew thyself approved unto God, a workman that needeth not to be ashamed, rightly dividing the word of truth.
> — 2 Timothy 2:15

1. *Charis* is the Greek word Paul used to describe the amazing, supernaturally given *grace* that God has provided us through His Spirit. What do we look like and what kinds of things are we enabled to do when we're operating in the Spirit with His grace? Consider the examples

of Peter and John in Acts 4:1-21; Stephen in Acts 7:55-60; and Paul in Acts 28:1-10.

2. The phrase "by the Spirit" carries the idea of *going back and forth in order to eventually cross over to the other side*. It is a picture of the Holy Spirit tirelessly working to bring you from a place of ignorance and confusion to one of clarity and understanding. Take a look at these examples from Scripture that illustrate this priceless work of God in our life. What stands out to you about these stories?

- **Moses: Exodus 3; 4:1-17**
- **Gideon: Judges 6**
- **Jonah: Jonah 1 and 2**
- **Paul: 2 Corinthians 12:7-10**

3. Name at least one area of *your* life where it is evident that the Holy Spirit has patiently worked to bring you from a place of ignorance and confusion to one of clarity and understanding.

PRACTICAL APPLICATION

> But be ye doers of the word, and not hearers only, deceiving your own selves.
> —James 1:22

1. In general, what do you think about speaking in tongues? Is there anything about it that makes you uneasy or fearful? If so, how has this lesson changed your view of what happens spiritually when you pray in your prayer language (tongues)?

2. The Bible declares, "…A person "speaking in tongues" helps himself grow spiritually…" (1 Corinthians 14:4 *TLB*). Therefore, it's no wonder God says, "But you, beloved, build yourselves up [founded] on your most holy faith [make progress, rise like an edifice higher and higher], praying in the Holy Spirit" (Jude 20 *AMPC*). Take time to pray and ask God to show you how you can begin to make praying in tongues more of a part of your daily life.

LESSON 3

TOPIC
A Prayer for Divine Revelation, Part 1

SCRIPTURES
1. **Ephesians 1:15-18** — Wherefore I also, after I heard of your faith in the Lord Jesus, and love unto all the saints, cease not to give thanks for you, making mention of you in my prayers; that the God of our Lord Jesus Christ, the Father of glory, may give unto you the spirit of wisdom and revelation in the knowledge of him: the eyes of your understanding being enlightened; that ye may know what is the hope of his calling, and what the riches of the glory of his inheritance in the saints.

GREEK WORDS
1. "cease not" — **οὐ παύομαι** (*ou pauomai*): the word **οὐ** (*ou*) means not, and the word **παύομαι** (*pauomai*) depicts the words to cease, to pause, or to stop and is where we get the word pause; here, it means I never cease, pause, stop, or take a break in giving thanks for you
2. "give thanks" — **εὐχαριστέω** (*eucharisteo*): to experience a generally good disposition or overwhelmingly good feeling about someone or something that causes one to experience and to express a free flow of gratitude or thankfulness
3. "for" — **ὑπὲρ** (*huper*): on your behalf; because of you
4. "making mention" — **ποιούμενος μνείαν** (*poioumenos mneian*): the word **ποιούμενος** (*poioumenos*) is a form of *poieo*, and the word **μνείαν** (*mneian*) is a form of **μνεία** (*mneia*); the word *poieo* means to create, to build, or to manufacture, and the word *mneia* pictures a monument, statue, or some type of memorial intended to be a permanent memorial to depict a person's actions or deeds
5. "in" — **ἐπὶ** (*epi*): on, upon, or on top
6. "that" — **ἵνα** (*hina*): points to an express purpose
7. "the Father" — **ὁ Πατὴρ** (*ho Pater*): the word **πατήρ** (*pater*) preceded by the definite article **ὁ** (*ho*); THE FATHER; portrays one who begets or imparts; a progenitor who produces and replicates

8. "glory" — δόξα (*doxa*): radiance, glory, splendor; the weightiness of God's presence that is filled with everything good
9. "may give" — δώῃ (*doe*): a form of δίδωμι (*didomi*); to give or to bestow as a gift; also means to supply or to furnish
10. "unto you" — ὑμῖν (*humin*): directly to you
11. "wisdom" — σοφία (*sophia*): in the New Testament, it usually depicts wisdom not naturally attained; special insight; it also portrays highly educated people, such as scientists, philosophers, doctors, teachers, and others who were considered to be the super-intelligentsia of society; those who are brilliant, intellectually sharp, or especially enlightened; a class of individuals whom the world would call clever, astute, smart, or intellectually brilliant; a term that was reserved for those considered to be intellectually impressive and a cut above the rest of society; here, we see that the impartation of σοφία (*sophia*) gives us such special insight that it raises us above the rest of society
12. "and" — καὶ (*kai*): even; a clarifying statement
13. "revelation" — ἀποκάλυψις (*apokalupsis*): from ἀποκαλύπτω (*apokalupto*), a compound of the preposition ἀπό (*apo*) and καλύπτω (*kalupto*); the preposition ἀπό (*apo*) means away, as to remove something, and the word καλύπτω (*kalupto*) means to conceal, as to hide or to obstruct; when compounded, it refers to something that has been veiled or hidden but then becomes clear and visible to the mind or eye; a sudden revealing; an unveiling or, thus, to uncover; because the veil has been removed, what is behind the veil is no longer concealed or hidden from view; a divine revelation; the ability to know, see, and understand what one could never know, see, and understand by himself
14. "knowledge" — ἐπίγνωσις (*epignosis*): compound of the preposition ἐπί (*epi*) and γινώσκω (*ginosko*); the preposition ἐπί (*epi*) here, is an intensifier, and γινώσκω (*ginosko*) means I know, I perceive, I realize, or I recognize and carries the idea of knowing by experience; compounded to form the word ἐπίγνωσις (*epignosis*), it depicts experiential knowledge, first-hand knowledge, or personal knowledge; it pictures one who is on top of his subject
15. "eyes" — ὀφθαλμός (*ophthalmos*): plural form of ὀφθαλμός (*ophthalmos*), the eyes

16. "understanding" — καρδίας (*kardias*): from καρδία (*kardia*), the human heart; thus, the central organ that pumps blood into all the body
17. "enlightened" — φωτίζω (*photidzo*): to lighten up; to illuminate; to shine; to radiate; gives the impression of a brilliant flash of light that leaves a permanent and lasting impression
18. "that" — εἰς (*eis*): into; progressing toward; leading into
19. "know" — οἶδα (*oida*): to comprehend, perceive, see, or understand
20. "what is" — τίς ἐστιν (*tis estin*): what is, exactly what is, or precisely what is
21. "what" — τίς (*tis*): exactly or precisely what is
22. "riches" — πλοῦτος (*ploutos*): immense wealth or riches beyond imagination; many riches; pictures one who possesses wealth so immense that it is immeasurable; abundant riches or measureless resources
23. "in" — ἐν (*en*): in; identifies the place where His inheritance is located

SYNOPSIS

Back in the Seventeenth Century, there was a real problem in Russia with people peeking into other people's windows. In fact, it was such an issue that homeowners across the country decided to create a distraction to draw people's attention, and therefore, they put forth great effort to trim their windows and even their roofs with colorful latticework. It seems that everyone was competing to see who could create the most whimsical and eye-catching designs. They thought if they could capture people's attention with their decorations it would keep them from peeking into their windows.

In some ways, our lives are like these highly decorated windows. Spiritually speaking, we have a lot of colorful "latticework" all around us that's distracting us from what is most important. Yet, God wants to give us divine revelation into the hidden mysteries He has placed deep inside of us. In this lesson, we will examine a prayer for divine revelation written by the apostle Paul in Ephesians 1.

The emphasis of this lesson:

God's glorious presence is filled with everything good, including His divine wisdom and revelation. When we receive His wisdom, we receive

supernatural insight that lifts us above the rest of society. It is God's desire that we have our eyes wide open and experience a personal, firsthand, heart revelation of Jesus.

Paul Was Very Thankful for the Believers in Ephesus

The church of Ephesus was the largest church in Asia, and Paul planted it with the help of his friends Aquila and Priscilla. When he wrote his letter to the believers there, he included a prayer for receiving divine revelation. Paul started off by saying, "Wherefore I also, after I heard of your faith in the Lord Jesus, and love unto all the saints, cease not to give thanks for you, making mention of you in my prayers" (Ephesians 1:15,16).

Notice the words "cease not," which begin verse 16. They are a translation of the Greek words *ou pauomai*. The word *ou* means *not* and is a *canceller*; and the word *pauomai* means *to cease, to pause*, or *to stop* and is where we get the word *pause*. Here, these words are the equivalent of Paul saying, "I never cease, pause, stop, or take a break in giving thanks for you."

When Paul said he "gives thanks," he inserted the Greek word *eucharisteo*, which means *to experience a generally good disposition or overwhelmingly good feeling about someone or something that causes one to experience and to express a free flow of gratitude or thankfulness*. The use of *eucharisteo* is the equivalent of Paul saying, "Ephesian saints, I love you so much, and when I think of you, I have such good feelings I don't even have to try to be thankful for you. I'm just naturally grateful for you, and my thankfulness freely flows out of my heart."

Our Prayers Build Memorials in God's Presence

Paul said he was constantly "making mention" of the Ephesian believers. This phrase is a translation of the Greek words *poioumenos mneian*. The word *poioumenos* is a form of *poieo* and means *to create, to build*, or *to manufacture*. The word *mneian* is a form of *mneia*, which pictures *a monument, statue*, or *some type of memorial intended to be a permanent memorial to depict a person's actions or deeds*.

So when Paul said he was "making mention" of the Ephesian believers in his prayers, he was basically telling them, "In my prayers, I'm fabricating, producing, and manufacturing statues, monuments, and memorials of you." This tells us that when we sincerely pray and express our gratefulness for others, our faith-filled words don't just leave our lips and disappear. Instead, they create monuments, statues, and memorials in the presence of God of the person for whom we're praying. And God sees the memorials of these precious people because of the prayers we have prayed.

An example of this is seen in the life of Cornelius, the Roman centurion who feared God, prayed continually, and gave offerings on behalf of the Jewish people. The Bible says that one day when Cornelius was praying, an angel came to him in a vision, "And when he [Cornelius] looked on him, he was afraid, and said, What is it, Lord? And he said unto him, Thy prayers and thine alms are come up for a *memorial* before God" (Acts 10:4). The word "memorial" here is a form of the same Greek word — *mneia*. In this case, Cornelius' own prayers had established a monument in the presence of God that moved Him to bring salvation to Cornelius and his entire family (*see* Acts 10).

So remember, when you pray as Paul did, *making mention* of people in your prayers, your faith-infused words don't just disappear — they literally ascend into the presence of God and build an eternal memorial or monument of that person and/or their need. God sees and is confronted by what you pray.

God's Glorious Presence Is Filled With Everything Good

In Ephesians 1:17, we are told more specifically what Paul prayed. He said, "That the God of our Lord Jesus Christ, the Father of glory, may give unto you the spirit of wisdom and revelation in the knowledge of him." The first word — "that" — is again the Greek word *hina*, and it points to *an express purpose*. It's the same as Paul saying, "Here is explicitly what I'm praying for you."

Paul's prayers were directed to "the Father," which is a translation of the Greek words *ho Pater* — the word *pater* preceded by the definite article *ho*. Hence, this is not just any father; it is "THE FATHER." This term portrays *one who begets or imparts; a progenitor who produces and replicates*. In this instance, Paul was pointing to THE FATHER who imparts, produces, and replicates "glory."

The word "glory" here is a form of the Greek word *doxa*, which describes the *radiance, glory,* or *splendor of God*. It also denotes *the weightiness of God's presence that is filled with everything good*. As the Father of glory, it is God's nature to produce glorious experiences and impart His glorious presence that is filled with everything good. When you have an encounter with the glory of God, it imparts something to you, which is why we need to be in gatherings where His glory is in manifestation.

Paul prayed that "...the Father of glory, may give unto you the spirit of wisdom and revelation..." (Ephesians 1:17). In Greek, the words "may give" is the term *doe*, a form of the word *didomi*, which means *to give or to bestow as a gift* or *to supply or furnish something*. And the phrase "unto you" is the word *humin*, which means *directly to you*. When you experience God's glory, it will supply and furnish directly to you a priceless gift right out of His glory.

Wisdom and Revelation Are Gifts From God

What does God want to give directly to you out of the weightiness of His presence? Paul said, "...the spirit of wisdom and revelation in the knowledge of him" (Ephesians 1:17). The word "wisdom" here is quite extraordinary. It is a form of the Greek word *sophia*, and in the New Testament, it usually depicts *wisdom not naturally attained*. Indeed, it is *special insight*, and in a secular sense, this Greek word — *sophia* — also portrays highly educated people, such as scientists, philosophers, doctors, teachers, and others who were considered to be the super-intelligentsia of society.

In general, it denotes those who are brilliant, intellectually sharp, or especially enlightened. This is a class of individuals whom the world would call clever, astute, smart, or intellectually brilliant. This term was reserved for those considered to be intellectually impressive and a cut above the rest of society. Here the apostle Paul uses this word to tell us that when we have an encounter with the glory of God, His glory touches us and imparts to us *sophia* (wisdom), which gives us such special insight that it raises us above the rest of society.

In addition to wisdom, Paul adds "and revelation." The word "and" here is the Greek word *kai*, which serves as a clarifying statement. A better translation of this would be, "May the Father of glory give you the gift and impart to you wisdom not naturally attained — *even revelation.*"

Interestingly, the word "revelation" is a form of the Greek word *apokalupsis*, which is derived from *apokalupto*, a compound of the words *apo* and *kalupto*. The preposition *apo* means *away*, as *to remove something*, and the word *kalupto* means *to conceal*, as *to hide* or *to obstruct*. When compounded, the new word *apokalupsis* refers to *something that has been veiled or hidden but then becomes clear and visible to the mind or eye*. It is *a sudden revealing*, *an unveiling*, or *an uncovering*, and because the veil has been removed, what was behind the veil is no longer concealed or hidden from view. Thus, Paul prayed for divine revelation to be granted to these believers — and us — giving them the ability to know, see, and understand what one could never know, see, and understand on their own.

Having a Personal Revelation of Jesus Is God's Desire

Along with a spirit of wisdom and revelation, Paul also prayed that the Ephesian believers would be blessed with "…the knowledge of him [Jesus]" (Ephesians 1:17). The word "knowledge" here is the remarkable Greek word *epignosis*, which is a compound of the preposition *epi* and *ginosko*. The word *epi* literally means *to be on top of*, and here, it serves as an intensifier. The word *ginosko* means *I know, I perceive, I realize*, or *I recognize* and carries the idea of *knowing by experience*. When compounded to form the word *epignosis*, it depicts *experiential knowledge, first-hand knowledge*, or *personal knowledge*. It is a picture of *one who is on top of his subject*.

So when Paul said he was praying, "That the God of our Lord Jesus Christ, the Father of glory, may give unto you the spirit of wisdom and revelation in the knowledge of him," he was saying, "I'm praying that the curtain will part and you will see and experience Jesus as you've never seen and experienced Him before — and that you have a firsthand, personal experience with Him to such a degree that, like a professional, you are on top of the subject when it comes to knowing the person of Christ."

To all of this, Paul prayed that "The eyes of your understanding being enlightened; that ye may know what is the hope of his calling, and what the riches of the glory of his inheritance in the saints" (Ephesians 1:18). The word "eyes" here is the Greek word *ophthalmos*, which is plural, signifying *the eyes*. The use of this word indicates that God wants you to have both your eyes wide open to receive the full revelation of who Jesus is.

When the Bible talks about the "eyes of your understanding," the word "understanding" is the Greek word *kardias*, which is from the word *kardia*, the term from where we get *cardiac*. It is the word for *the human heart*, the central organ that pumps blood into every part of the body.

Paul prayed that the eyes of our *heart* — the very core of who we are — would be "enlightened." This word is a form of the Greek word *photidzo*, and it means *to lighten up, to illuminate, to shine*, or *to radiate*. This word gives the impression of *a brilliant flash of light that leaves a permanent and lasting impression*. Thus, Paul was praying that just as our heart pumps blood to every part of our body, the core of our spirit man would begin to "pump" revelation to every part of who we are.

Understanding the Hope of Jesus Is Like Immeasurable Riches

Why is this enlightenment so vital? Paul wrote, "…That ye may know what is the hope of his calling, and what the riches of the glory of his inheritance in the saints" (Ephesians 1:18). In this verse, the opening word "that" is the Greek word *eis*, which means *into* and signifies *a leading into something*. With God, there is always a progression toward new understanding.

This brings us to the word "know," which in Greek is *oida*. It means *to comprehend, to perceive, to see*, or *to understand*. God wants each of us to comprehend and see more and more "what is the hope of his calling." The phrase "what is" is a translation of the Greek words *tis estin*, and it means *what is, exactly what is*, or *precisely what is*. This demonstrates how much God wants us to be on top of the subject of who Jesus is. He wants to reveal to us everything down to the most minute detail "…what is the hope of his calling, and what the riches of the glory of his inheritance in the saints" (Ephesians 1:18).

In Greek, the word "riches" is *ploutos*, and it describes *immense wealth or riches beyond imagination*. Moreover, it pictures *many riches* and *one who possesses wealth so immense that it is immeasurable*. Indeed, personally experiencing the glory of Jesus is *abundant riches* or *measureless resources*. Paul noted that these immense riches are "in the saints." The word "in" in Greek is *en*, which means *in*, but more importantly, it identifies the place where His inheritance is located — *within the saints*, which is the Church.

In our next lesson, we will continue focusing on a prayer for divine revelation.

STUDY QUESTIONS

> Study to shew thyself approved unto God, a workman that
> needeth not to be ashamed, rightly dividing the word of truth.
> — 2 Timothy 2:15

1. As we have noted throughout the first three lessons, our lives are often surrounded by elaborate distractions that make it hard to focus on Jesus. To help you overcome this dilemma, take time to meditate on Hebrews 12:1 and 2 in a few Bible versions. What is the Holy Spirit showing you from these scriptures? What action(s) do you sense Him prompting you to take?
2. When it comes to knowing Jesus, God wants to give you a personal, firsthand experience that makes you a professional of the subject. According to Jeremiah 29:12,13 and Deuteronomy 4:29, what is the basis of seeking and knowing God? What does Jesus say about knowing and learning about Him in Matthew 11:28-30 and in John 16:13-15? (Also consider First John 4:7-17.)
3. To know Jesus is to know wisdom! How do Colossians 2:2 and 3 and First Corinthians 1:30 confirm this powerful principle?

PRACTICAL APPLICATION

> But be ye doers of the word, and not hearers only,
> deceiving your own selves.
> — James 1:22

1. Divine revelation is one of God's greatest gifts to us — it makes truth clear and our path straight when we have questions. What's one area of your life where you really need God to pull back the curtains and reveal things?
2. Amazingly, our prayers don't evaporate after they leave our lips. Instead, they build monuments and memorials in God's presence that are always in His line of sight. How does knowing this encourage you? What people or situations are you grateful to know God hasn't forgotten? Who or what do you feel inspired to begin praying about?

LESSON 4

TOPIC
A Prayer for Divine Revelation, Part 2

SCRIPTURES
1. **Ephesians 1:17-19** — That the God of our Lord Jesus Christ, the Father of glory, may give unto you the spirit of wisdom and revelation in the knowledge of him: The eyes of your understanding being enlightened; that ye may know what is the hope of his calling, and what the riches of the glory of his inheritance in the saints, and what is the exceeding greatness of his power to us-ward who believe, according to the working of his mighty power.

GREEK WORDS
1. "that" — ἵνα (*hina*): points to an express purpose
2. "the Father" — ὁ Πατὴρ (*ho Pater*): the word πατήρ (*pater*) preceded by the definite article ὁ (*ho*); THE FATHER; portrays one who begets or imparts; a progenitor who produces and replicates
3. "glory" — δόξα (*doxa*): radiance, glory, splendor; the weightiness of God's presence that is filled with everything good
4. "may give" — δώῃ (*doe*): a form of δίδωμι (*didomi*) to give or to bestow as a gift; also means to supply or to furnish
5. "unto you" — ὑμῖν (*humin*): directly to you
6. "wisdom" — σοφία (*sophia*): in the New Testament, it usually depicts wisdom not naturally attained; special insight; it also portrays highly educated people, such as scientists, philosophers, doctors, teachers, and others who were considered to be the super-intelligentsia of society; those who are brilliant, intellectually sharp, or especially enlightened; a class of individuals whom the world would call clever, astute, smart, or intellectually brilliant; a term that was reserved for those considered to be intellectually impressive and a cut above the rest of society; here, we see that the impartation of σοφία (*sophia*) gives us such special insight that it raises us above the rest of society
7. "and" — καὶ (*kai*): even; a clarifying statement

8. "revelation" — ἀποκάλυψις (*apokalupsis*): from ἀποκαλύπτω (*apokalupto*), a compound of the preposition ἀπό (*apo*) and καλύπτω (*kalupto*); the preposition ἀπό (*apo*) means away, as to remove something, and the word καλύπτω (*kalupto*) means to conceal, as to hide or to obstruct; when compounded, it refers to something that has been veiled or hidden but then becomes clear and visible to the mind or eye; a sudden revealing; an unveiling or, thus, to uncover; because the veil has been removed, what is behind the veil is no longer concealed or hidden from view; a divine revelation; the ability to know, see, and understand what one could never know, see, and understand by himself

9. "knowledge" — ἐπίγνωσις (*epignosis*): compound of the preposition ἐπί (*epi*) and γινώσκω (*ginosko*); the preposition ἐπί (*epi*) here, is an intensifier, and γινώσκω (*ginosko*) means I know, I perceive, I realize, or I recognize and carries the idea of knowing by experience; compounded to form the word ἐπίγνωσις (*epignosis*), it depicts experiential knowledge, first-hand knowledge, or personal knowledge; it pictures one who is on top of his subject

10. "eyes" — ὀφθαλμὸς (*ophthalmos*): plural form of ὀφθαλμὸς (*ophthalmos*), the eyes

11. "understanding" — καρδίας (*kardias*): from καρδία (*kardia*), the human heart; thus, the central organ that pumps blood into all the body

12. "enlightened" — φωτίζω (*photidzo*): to lighten up; to illuminate; to shine; to radiate; gives the impression of a brilliant flash of light that leaves a permanent and lasting impression

13. "that" — εἰς (*eis*): into; progressing toward; leading into

14. "know" — οἶδα (*oida*): to comprehend, perceive, see, or understand

15. "what is" — τίς ἐστιν (*tis estin*): what is, exactly what is, or precisely what is

16. "the hope" — ἡ ἐλπὶς (*he elpis*): the word ἐλπὶς (*elpis*) with the definite article ἡ (*he*); hence, not just a hope, but THE hope; not a hope-so kind of hope, but an anticipation and an expectation that the thing hoped for will certainly come to pass; pictures Christ's firm assurance that His calling will be fulfilled

17. "his calling" — τῆς κλήσεως αὐτοῦ (*tes kleseos autou*): the calling of him, or his calling; the word κλήσεως (*kleseos*) is a form of κλητός (*kletos*); conveys the idea of those called or invited to an event that was

normally closed to the public and, thus, an event that one could only participate in by a VIP invitation; used to describe a special invitation extended by a king who asked people to attend a feast; such royal events were closed to the public so a person couldn't attend without being invited; receiving an invitation to attend this type of special occasion was therefore considered an honor to be treasured, prized, and revered; here, it pictures the magnificent calling that the Father extended to Christ

18. "what" — τίς (*tis*): exactly or precisely what is
19. "riches" — πλοῦτος (*ploutos*): immense wealth or riches beyond imagination; many riches; pictures one who possesses wealth so immense that it is immeasurable; abundant riches or measureless resources
20. "glory of his inheritance" — τῆς δόξης τῆς κληρονομίας αὐτοῦ (*tes doxes tes kleronomias autou*): this phrase is intended to show how glorious, splendid, and weighty is His inheritance
21. "in" — ἐν (*en*): in; identifies the place where His inheritance is located
22. "what is" — τί (*ti*): points to the most minute detail; down-to-the-smallest-detail type of knowledge
23. "exceeding" — ὑπερβάλλω (*huperballo*): a compound of the preposition ὑπέρ (*huper*) and βάλλω (*ballo*); the preposition ὑπέρ (*huper*) describes something that is above and beyond what is normal or something that is exceeding or surpassing; the word βάλλω (*ballo*) means to hurl or to throw; when compounded, the word ὑπερβάλλω (*huperballo*) pictures something like an archer who aims his arrow at the target but shoots way over the top of it; hence, it depicts something beyond the range of anything considered normal or something that is unparalleled
24. "greatness" — μέγεθος (*megethos*): greatness, immensity, limitlessness, or vastness
25. "of his power" — τῆς δυνάμεως αὐτοῦ (*tes dunameos autou*): literally, of the power of Him; but the δυνάμεως (*dunameos*) is a form of δύναμις (*dunamis*), which denotes explosive, superhuman power that comes with enormous energy and produces phenomenal, extraordinary, and unparalleled results; depicts "mighty deeds" that are impressive, incomparable, and beyond human ability to perform; miraculous power or miraculous manifestations; the same word used to denote a force of nature like a hurricane, tornado, or an earthquake
26. "to" — εἰς (*eis*): into; carries the idea of progression

27. "us-ward" — ἡμᾶς (*hemas*): directly to us
28. "who believe" — τοὺς πιστεύοντας (*tous pisteuontas*): literally, to the ones who are believing; denotes those whose faith is activated and engaged in a state of believing
29. "according to" — κατά (*kata*): a preposition that can be translated according to, but importantly carries the sense of a dominating and subjugating force; hence, being dominated and subjugated by
30. "the working" — τὴν ἐνέργειαν (*ten energeian*): from ἐνέργεια (*energeia*) with a definite article; not simply a working, but THE working; the word ἐνέργεια (*energeia*) is power in action; one scholar states ἐνέργεια (*energeia*) refers to God's divine and supernatural energy to transition a believer from point to point in His plan
31. "of his mighty power" — τοῦ κράτους τῆς ἰσχύος αὐτοῦ (*tou kratous ischuos autou*): literally, of the power of the might of Him; however, here we find a form of κράτος (*kratos*), which is not merely power, but demonstrated or visible power; a power that is eruptive and tangible; thus, this is not hypothetical power but real power that is overpowering and irresistible; in this phrase is also a form of ἰσχύος (*ischuos*), which pictures a strong man or a man with great muscular capabilities; in the New Testament, it pictures God as One who is able, mighty, and muscular or One with all the ability and might to overcome any foe or to accomplish any act needed

SYNOPSIS

To receive wisdom from God is to see into the windows of Heaven and receive divine revelation through the agency of His Holy Spirit. Many times, God wants to reveal new and powerful things to us, but we are too distracted by the trappings and cares of this life — much like the Russian people were distracted by the colorful latticework that surrounded the windows of people's homes.

God said, "…Call to me and I will answer you. I'll tell you marvelous and wondrous things that you could never figure out on your own" (Jeremiah 33:3 *MSG*). If you'll remove the distractions from your life and seek the presence of God, the Holy Spirit will remove the veil to the spirit realm and show you great and mighty things you've never seen before!

The emphasis of this lesson:

Paul prayed for divine revelation to be granted to all believers, giving us the ability to see and understand what we can't see and understand on our own. God wants us to know the hope of Christ's calling, the glory of His inheritance, the exceeding greatness of His power, and the working of His mighty power to all who believe.

A Review of Lesson 3

The Father Wants You To Experience the Fullness of His Glory. The apostle Paul opens Ephesians 1:17 with the word "that," which is the Greek word *hina*, and it points to *an express purpose*. This word is the equivalent of Paul saying, "I am explicitly praying for you that...." In this case, he was specifically praying "*That* the God of our Lord Jesus Christ, the Father of glory, may give unto you the spirit of wisdom and revelation in the knowledge of him" (Ephesians 1:17).

We noted that Paul's prayers were directed to "the Father," which is a translation of the Greek words *ho Pater*. The word *pater* means *father*, but in this verse, it is preceded by the definite article *ho*. So this is not just any father; it is "THE FATHER." The word *pater* pictures *one who begets or imparts; a progenitor who produces and replicates*. This tells us that our Heavenly Father wants to impart, produce, and replicate something in our lives — it is His "glory."

This word "glory" is a form of the Greek word *doxa*, which describes *the radiance, glory,* or *splendor of God*. It also depicts *the weightiness of God's presence that is filled with everything good*. As the Father of glory, it is God's desire to produce glorious experiences and impart His glorious presence into your life. In fact, Paul prays that the Father of glory would give "unto you," which in Greek means *directly to you*. When you have an encounter with God's glory, it imparts something magnificent directly to you.

Specifically, Paul prayed that "...the Father of glory, may give unto you the spirit of wisdom and revelation..." (Ephesians 1:17). The words "may give" are a translation of the word *doe*, a form of the word *didomi*, which means *to give or to bestow as a gift; to supply or fully furnish*. This lets us know that God really wants to supply and furnish directly to you the weightiness of His glory, which is filled with everything good.

He Desires To Impart His Wisdom and Revelation. Two indescribable blessings God wants to supply directly to you are "the spirit of wisdom and revelation" (Ephesians 1:17). In Greek, the word "wisdom" is a form of the word *sophia*, and in the New Testament, it usually depicts *wisdom not naturally attained*. It can also be translated as *special insight*. This word *sophia* was used to portray highly educated people like scientists, philosophers, doctors, teachers, and others who were considered to be the super-intelligentsia of society.

Furthermore, the word *sophia* denotes those who are brilliant, intellectually sharp, or especially enlightened. This class of individuals was comprised of people whom the world would call clever, astute, smart, or intellectually brilliant. This term was reserved for those considered to be intellectually impressive and a cut above the rest of society. Here, the apostle Paul uses this word to tell us that when we have an encounter with the glory of God, His glory touches us and imparts to us *sophia* (wisdom). And when His wisdom is operating in our lives, it elevates us above the rest of society.

Along with wisdom, Paul adds "and revelation." In Greek, the word "and" is the word *kai*, which serves as a clarifying statement. A better translation of this would be, "May the Father of glory give you the spirit of wisdom — *even revelation*." Again, this is wisdom not naturally attained — it is supernaturally imparted from God.

We saw that the word "revelation" is a translation of the Greek word *apokalupsis*, which is from *apokalupto*, a compound of the words *apo* and *kalupto*. The preposition *apo* means *away*, as *to remove something*, and the word *kalupto* means *to conceal* or *to hide something*. When these words come together to form *apokalupsis*, it describes *something that has been veiled or hidden but then becomes clear and visible to the mind or eye*. It is *a sudden revealing* or *an unveiling*, and because the veil has been removed, what was concealed is no longer hidden from view. Thus, Paul prayed for divine revelation to be granted to believers, giving all of us the ability to know, see, and understand what we couldn't know, see, and understand on our own.

He Wants the Eyes of Your Heart Wide Open. Paul continues in Ephesians 1:18 praying that "The eyes of your understanding being enlightened; that ye may know what is the hope of his calling, and what the riches of the glory of his inheritance in the saints." The word "eyes" in Greek is the word *ophthalmos*, and it is plural, indicating *the eyes*. This lets us know that God wants us to have both eyes wide open to receive the full revelation of who Jesus is.

Interestingly, when the Scripture talks about the "eyes of your understanding being enlightened," the word for "understanding" in Greek is *kardias*, which is from the word *kardia*, the term for *the human heart*. If you think about it, the heart is the central organ that pumps blood into every part of the body. Paul prayed that the eyes of our heart — meaning the core of who we are — would be "enlightened."

In Greek, the word "enlightened" is a form of the word *photidzo*, which means *to lighten up, to illuminate, to shine*, or *to radiate*. This word *photidzo* also describes *a brilliant flash of light that leaves a permanent and lasting impression*. Basically, Paul is praying that we would have such a spirit of wisdom and revelation at the very core of our being that our heart would be filled with light. And as our natural heart pumps blood to our entire body, he's praying that our spiritual heart would begin to pump revelation into every area of our life until we are filled with divine enlightenment.

To Know the Hope of His Calling. The reason for having the eyes of your heart illuminated is "…that ye may know what is the hope of his calling, and what the riches of the glory of his inheritance in the saints" (Ephesians 1:18). In this verse, the word "that" is the Greek word *eis*, which means *into*, and here it carries the idea of an experience that is progressive — it is *leading you forward into something*. In this case, God's Spirit is leading you to "know what is the hope of his calling."

In Greek, the word "know" here is *oida*, and it always means *to comprehend, to perceive, to see*, or *to understand*. God wants all of us to see and understand "what is the hope of his calling." When you read this in Greek, the words "what is" are a translation of *tis estin*, which means *what is, exactly what is*, or *precisely what is*. This verse shows us that God wants to give us a revelation so precise that we know exactly "what is the hope of His calling." The calling being referred to here is the assignment the Father gave to Jesus.

'The Hope of His Calling'

Now, you may be wondering, *What is the hope of his calling?* First, let's look at the words "the hope," which are *he elpis* in Greek. It is a combination of the word *elpis* with the definite article *he*. Hence, this is not just *any old* hope, but THE hope. Likewise, it's not a hope-so kind of hope, but an anticipation and an expectation that the thing hoped for will certainly come to pass. Here, it pictures Christ's firm assurance that His calling will be fulfilled.

Next, notice the phrase "his calling," which is *tes kleseos autou* in Greek. In the original text, it literally says *the calling of him*, meaning *his calling*. It is from the word *kleseos*, which is a form of *kletos* and conveys the idea of *those called or invited to an event that was normally closed to the public*. Thus, it was an event that one could only participate in by a VIP invitation.

Moreover, this word *kleseos* was used to describe *a special invitation extended by a king who asked people to attend a feast*. Such royal events were closed to the public, so a person couldn't attend without being invited. Receiving an invitation to attend this type of special occasion was therefore considered an honor to be treasured, prized, and revered. In Ephesians 1:18, the word *kleseos* pictures the magnificent calling that the Father extended to Christ. It is the highest calling that Jesus fully anticipated fulfilling.

'The Glory of His Inheritance'

The apostle Paul also prayed that we come to know "…what the riches of the glory of his inheritance in the saints" (Ephesians 1:18). The phrase "what" in Greek is *tis*, and it means *exactly* or *precisely what is*. The word "riches" is the Greek word *ploutos*, which describes *immense wealth* or *riches beyond imagination*. It pictures *one who possesses wealth so immense that it is immeasurable*. These are abundant riches or measureless resources.

Paul then specifies that these riches are the "glory of his inheritance," which in Greek is a phrase intended to show how glorious, splendid, and weighty is His inheritance, and that inheritance is "in the saints." The word "in" here is the little Greek word *en*, and it identifies the place where His inheritance is located — *inside the saints*, which is in the Church.

'The Exceeding Greatness of His Power'

In addition to understanding the riches of Christ's glorious inheritance, Paul also prayed that we would comprehend "…what is the exceeding greatness of his power to us-ward who believe, according to the working of his mighty power" (Ephesians 1:19). Notice for a third time in two verses that the words "what is" (or "what") appear. Here, it is the little

Greek word *ti*, and it points to *the most minute detail, down-to-the-smallest-detail type of knowledge.*

God wants to give you a revelation of "the exceeding greatness of His power." The word "greatness" here is *megethos*, which describes *greatness, immensity, limitlessness,* or *vastness,* and the word "exceeding" is a form of the Greek word *huperballo,* a compound of the preposition *huper* and *ballo*. The word *huper* describes *something that is above and beyond what is normal* or *something that is exceeding or surpassing*. The word *ballo* means *to hurl* or *to throw*. When compounded, the word *huperballo* pictures something like an archer who aims his arrow at the target but shoots way over the top of it. Hence, it depicts *something beyond the range of anything considered normal* or *something that is unparalleled*. This is the kind of power God has made available to you.

The phrase "of his power" is *tes dunameos autou* in Greek, which literally means *of the power of him*. The word *dunameos* is a form of *dunamis,* which denotes *explosive, superhuman power that comes with enormous energy and produces phenomenal, extraordinary, and unparalleled results.* Here it depicts "mighty deeds" that are impressive, incomparable, and beyond human ability to perform. *Dunameos* is the very word translated as *miraculous power* or *miraculous manifestations*. It is the same word used to denote *a force of nature like a hurricane, tornado,* or *an earthquake*. The use of this word means that God has explosive, superhuman power available, and when that power operates in us, it turns us into a spiritual force of nature that produces earth-changing results. God wants to give you a revelation of that power.

His Power Is Released Directly to Those Who Believe

Paul then clarified that this extraordinary power is "to us-ward." The word "to" is the Greek word *eis,* meaning *into* and carries the idea of *progression.* "Us-ward" in Greek is *hemas* and indicates *directly to us*. So, the exceeding greatness of his power is released directly to us "who believe." In Greek, the words "who believe" are a translation of *tous pisteuontas,* which literally means *to the ones who are believing*. The tense here denotes those whose faith is activated and engaged in a state of believing. Actively believing what God has said is required to release His power.

And the loosing of this explosive, superhuman ability is "according to the working of His mighty power." The words "according to" are a translation of the Greek word *kata*, a preposition that can be translated *according to*, but importantly carries the sense of *a dominating and subjugating force*. Hence, it pictures being dominated and subjugated by "the working of His mighty power."

In Greek, "the working" is *ten energeian*, which is from the word *energeia* but with the definite article *ten*. Thus, it is not simply *a* working, but THE working. The word *energeia* is *power in action*. One scholar states *energeia* refers to God's divine and supernatural energy to transition a believer from point to point in His plan.

His Mighty Power Is Tangible and Eruptive

This takes us to the closing phrase of Ephesians 1:19 — "of his mighty power." It is a translation of the Greek words *tou kratous ischuos autou*, which literally means *of the power of the might of him*. Here, we find a form of the word *kratos*, which is not merely power but *demonstrated or visible power, a power that is eruptive and tangible*. Thus, this is not hypothetical power but real power that is consuming and irresistible.

In this phrase, there is also a form of the word *ischuos*. Here, it is translated as "might," and it pictures *a strong man* or *a man with great muscular capabilities*. We could say this is like Mr. Universe who is covered with muscles. In the New Testament, it pictures God as One who is able, mighty, and muscular — One with all the ability and might to overcome any foe or accomplish any act needed.

This verse tells us God's mighty power is available to us, and when that mighty power begins to flow into us, it's not just mental or theoretical power; it is real, tangible, demonstrated power. It is eruptive power that you can personally feel and experience.

Friend, if you're not experiencing God's tangible power on a daily basis, begin to pray this prayer outlined in Ephesians 1:17-19 regularly. Jesus loves you and wants you to experience all that He has provided to you! In our final lesson, we will move to Ephesians 3 and explore Paul's prayer for divine comprehension.

STUDY QUESTIONS

> Study to shew thyself approved unto God, a workman that needeth not to be ashamed, rightly dividing the word of truth.
> — 2 Timothy 2:15

1. Ephesians 1:18 tells us that the riches of God's glory — Christ's inheritance — is located inside the saints, which is in us, the Church. What riches are you aware of that have been deposited in you? Consider John 14:27; 15:11; Romans 5:5; Second Corinthians 5:21; and Galatians 4:6; 5:22,23.

2. Another aspect of the riches of Christ's inheritance is the gifts and talents He's entrusted to us (*see* Matthew 25:14-30). Do you know what these are in your life? In what specific way has God designed and equipped you to bring Him glory? How are you stewarding Christ's inheritance? What adjustments might you make to be an even better manager of what He's given to you?

3. According to Ephesians 1:19, "the exceeding greatness of God's power" is available to you every moment of every day! The question is, how do you tap into it? Carefully read Jesus' words in John 15:1-8 and God's promise in Isaiah 40:28-31. What is the Holy Spirit showing you about accessing His power in these passages?

PRACTICAL APPLICATION

> But be ye doers of the word, and not hearers only, deceiving your own selves.
> — James 1:22

1. When the Bible talks about the hope of His calling, the word "calling" refers to those called or invited to a private event that was normally closed to the public. How does knowing you have a VIP invitation to join God's family through Jesus fill you with hope? Did you know you had this kind of acceptance from God?

2. Are you experiencing God's tangible, visible power regularly? If not, would you like to? If yes, then pray this personalized version of Paul's prayer found in Ephesians 1:17-19:

   Father, I pray that You would impart to me Your glorious presence, filled with everything good. Supply and fully furnish me with Your divine wisdom — even revelation. Pull back the curtain and show me spiritual mysteries, enabling me to see and understand what I could never see and understand on my own. May the eyes of my heart be wide open and illuminated to grasp precisely what is THE hope of Christ's calling and exactly what is the immeasurable riches of His inheritance in me. Give me a detailed understanding of His immense, unparalleled power that's like a force of nature, producing extraordinary, superhuman results. Thank You, Father, for releasing Your explosive, supernatural energy and might in and through my life in tangible ways. I love You, Father. In Jesus' name. Amen.

LESSON 5

TOPIC
Paul's Prayer for Divine Comprehension

SCRIPTURES

1. **Ephesians 3:14-19** — For this cause I bow my knees unto the Father of our Lord Jesus Christ, of whom the whole family in heaven and earth is named, that he would grant you, according to the riches of his glory, to be strengthened with might by his Spirit in the inner man; That Christ may dwell in your hearts by faith; that ye, being rooted and grounded in love, May be able to comprehend with all saints what is the breadth, and length, and depth, and height; And to know the love of Christ, which passeth knowledge, that ye might be filled with all the fulness of God.

GREEK WORDS

1. "bow" — **κάμπτω** (*kampto*): I bow, I bend
2. "knees" — **τὰ γόνατά** (*ta gonata*): plural, knees
3. "that" — **ἵνα** (*hina*): points to an express purpose
4. "grant" — **δῷ** (*do*): a form of **δίδωμι** (*didomi*); to give or to bestow as a gift; to supply or to furnish
5. "you" — **ὑμῖν** (*humin*): directly to you

6. "according to" — **κατά** (*kata*): a preposition that can be translated according to, but importantly carries the sense of a dominating and subjugating force; hence, being dominated and subjugated by
7. "the riches" — **πλοῦτος** (*ploutos*): immense wealth or riches beyond imagination; many riches; pictures one who possesses wealth so immense that it is immeasurable; abundant riches or measureless resources
8. "of his glory" — **τῆς δόξης αὐτοῦ** (*tes doxes auto*): literally, of the glory of Him; His glory; intended to show how glorious, splendid, and weighty is His glory
9. "to be strengthened with might" — **δυνάμει κραταιωθῆναι** (*dunamei krataiothenai*): from **δύναμις** (*dunamis*) and **κράτος** (*kratos*); the word **δύναμις** (*dunamis*) denotes explosive, superhuman power that comes with enormous energy and produces phenomenal, extraordinary, and unparalleled results; depicts "mighty deeds" that are impressive, incomparable, and beyond human ability to perform; miraculous power or miraculous manifestations; the same word used to denote a force of nature like a hurricane, tornado, or an earthquake; the word **κράτος** (*kratos*) is demonstrated or visible power; a power that is eruptive and tangible; thus, this is not hypothetical power but real power that is irresistible and overpowering
10. "by" — **διά** (*dia*): by or through; indicates agency and instrumentality; carries the idea of going back and forth in order to go all the way through, as one who crosses to the other side; here, we find the never-give-up work of the Spirit to produce the power of God in us
11. "in" — **εἰς** (*eis*): into; indicates where this work is taking place and that it is ongoing and progressive
12. "inner" — **ἔσω** (*eso*): inner; interior; inside
13. "dwell" — **κατοικέω** (*katoikeo*): a compound of **κατά** (*kata*) and **οἰκέω** (*oikeo*); the preposition **κατά** (*kata*) means down, and the word **οἰκέω** (*oikeo*) means I dwell, I live, or I reside; compounded, it depicts settling down and being established in a new home and making oneself feel comfortable there; used to describe permanent residents
14. "in" — **ἐν** (*en*): in; identifies the place where Christ lives by His Spirit
15. "hearts" — **καρδίας** (*kardias*): from **καρδία** (*kardia*), the human heart; thus, the central organ that pumps blood into all the body
16. "by" — **διά** (*dia*): by or through; indicates agency and instrumentality
17. "that" — **ἵνα** (*hina*): points to an express purpose

18. "in love" — ἐν ἀγάπῃ (*en agape*): in love
19. "rooted" — ῥιζόω (*rhidzoo*): deeply rooted; a plant with deep roots
20. "grounded" — θεμελιόω (*themelioo*): established, like a solid, strong foundation upon which a mighty structure can be built
21. "may" — ἵνα (*hina*): points to an express purpose
22. "able" — ἐξισχύω (*exischuo*): a compound of ἐκ (*ek*) and ἰσχύω (*ischuo*); the preposition ἐκ (*ek*) means out, and ἰσχύω (*ischuo*) pictures strength and is derived from ἰσχύος (*ischuos*), which pictures a strong man or a man with great muscular capabilities; here, it pictures the strength deposited in the inner man of believers; literally means may be able to draw out or extract from that indwelling might
23. "to comprehend" — καταλαμβάνω (*katalambano*): to seize; to grab hold of; to pull down; to tackle; to conquer; to master; to hold under one's power
24. "with" — σὺν (*sun*): in partnership; this should be equally experienced by all saints
25. "what is" — τί (*ti*): points to the most minute detail; down-to-the-smallest-detail type of knowledge
26. "breadth" — πλάτος (*platos*): breadth; used to describe the farthest ends of the earth, hence, the farthest expanse
27. "length" — μῆκος (*mekos*): length; used to depict greatness
28. "height" — ὕψος (*hupsos*): height; what is elevated; eminence
29. "depth" — βάθος (*bathos*): the deepest parts of the sea; can denote deep thoughts, deep spiritual truths, or deeply laid plans
30. "know" — γνῶναί (*gnonai*): from γινώσκω (*ginosko*), meaning I know, I perceive, I realize, or I recognize and carries the idea of knowing by experience
31. "love" — ἀγάπη (*agape*): divine love
32. "passeth" — ὑπερβάλλω (*huperballo*): a compound of the preposition ὑπέρ (*huper*) and βάλλω (*ballo*); the preposition ὑπέρ (*huper*) describes something that is above and beyond what is normal or something that is exceeding or surpassing; the word βάλλω (*ballo*) means to hurl or to throw; when compounded, the word ὑπερβάλλω (*huperballo*) pictures something like an archer who aims his arrow at the target but shoots way over the top of it; hence, it depicts something beyond the range of anything considered normal or something that is unparalleled

33. "might be filled" — **πληρωθῆτε** (*plerothete*): from **πληρόω** (*pleroo*), to be completely filled; to fill completely; filled to the point of overflowing
34. "with" — **εἰς** (*eis*): into; indicates this work is ongoing and progressive
35. "all" — **πᾶν** (*pan*): all; all-inclusive; leaving nothing out
36. "fulness" — **πλήρωμα** (*pleroma*): sum total; fullness; super abundance

SYNOPSIS

Back in the Seventeenth Century, some people had a bad habit of peeking into other people's windows to see what was in their houses. To deal with this dilemma, homeowners began to say, "If we elaborately embellish our windows, maybe people will become so fixated on the decorations that they'll stop peeking through our windows to look into our houses." Amazingly, their idea worked and caught on among the rich and poor alike. People became so fascinated with all the peripheral decorations that they stopped looking through people's windows.

In a spiritual sense, we are often hindered from seeing what God wants to show us because of all the distractions in our lives. Let's face it: it's easy to become fixated on everything going on around us — both good and bad. But if we'll heed God's words — "Looking away [from all that will distract] to Jesus, Who is the Leader and the Source of our faith…" (Hebrews 12:2 *AMPC*) — He'll give us the ability to see and understand amazing things. In fact, He'll enable us to comprehend the height, the breadth, the width, and the depth of His indescribable love, which is the greatest revelation He has waiting.

The emphasis of this lesson:

Paul's prayer for believers is that we're dominated by the riches of Christ's glory; strengthened in our inner man by the might of His Spirit; desirous to let Christ permanently dwell in our hearts; and growing in our understanding and experience of His love. The longer we walk with the Lord, the more powerful we become in our spirit.

PAUL PRAYED FOR ALL BELIEVERS…
To Be Dominated by Christ's Glory

Continuing his letter to the believers in Ephesus, the apostle Paul wrote, "For this cause I bow my knees unto the Father of our Lord Jesus Christ, of whom the whole family in heaven and earth is named" (Ephesians 3:14,15). When Paul says, "I bow my knees," the word "bow" is the Greek word *kampto*, which means *I bow* or *I bend*, and the word "knees" in Greek is *ta gonata*, which is plural and depicts *knees*. Thus, Paul is telling us that he didn't just get down on one knee before God but both knees. It is a good and healthy practice to take time to bow low and worship the Lord on our knees.

While down on his knees, Paul prayed, "That he [God] would grant you, according to the riches of his glory, to be strengthened with might by his Spirit in the inner man" (Ephesians 3:16). Once again, Paul inserts the word "that" at the opening of the verse. It is the Greek word *hina*, and it points to *an express purpose*. It is as if he is saying, "I'm going to tell you explicitly what I'm praying for, and here it is: That He would grant you, according to the riches of His glory, to be strengthened with might by His Spirit in the inner man" (Ephesians 3:16).

The word "grant" here is the Greek word *do*, a form of *didomi*, which means *to give* or *to bestow as a gift*; *to supply* or *to furnish*. And the word "you" is *humin*, meaning *directly to you*. Thus, Paul isn't just praying for a mere touch from God — he is asking the Father to give an ample supply of something to believers, "according to the riches of His glory."

In Greek, the words "according to" are a form of the word *kata*, a preposition that can be translated *according to*, but it also carries the sense of *a dominating and subjugating force*. Hence, it is a request by Paul for believers to be dominated and controlled by something, and Ephesians 3:16 reveals this is the "riches of his glory."

"The riches" in Greek is the word *ploutos*, and it describes *immense wealth or riches beyond imagination*. It is a picture of *one who possesses wealth so immense that it is immeasurable*. These *abundant riches* or *measureless resources* are "of His glory," which in Greek literally means *of the glory of Him*. It is *His glory*, intended to show how *glorious, splendid, and weighty is His glory*. Thus, God doesn't want you to experience just a small taste of His glory — He wants to fully furnish you directly with such a rich supply that you're dominated by His glory.

To Be Strengthened With His Might

Also in Paul's prayer is a request that believers "be strengthened with might" (Ephesians 3:16). This phrase is a translation of the Greek words *dunamei krataiothenai*, which is from *dunamis* and *kratos*. The word *dunamis* denotes *explosive, superhuman power that comes with enormous energy and produces phenomenal, extraordinary, and unparalleled results*. It is the New Testament word depicting "mighty deeds" that are impressive, incomparable, and beyond human ability to perform. Additionally, the word *dunamis* depicts *miraculous power* or *miraculous manifestations*, and it is the same word used to describe *a force of nature like a hurricane, tornado,* or *an earthquake*.

If we stop right there, this verse tells us that when we have an experience with the glory of God, it somehow produces and strengthens within us dynamic power that is explosive, superhuman, and generates extraordinary, unparalleled results. It transforms us into a one-man army, advancing forward to take territory. Furthermore, we become like a force of nature that stirs and shakes things up like a spiritual hurricane, tornado, or earthquake. All this meaning is found in the word *dunamis*.

The second Greek word which makes up the phrase "be strengthened with might" is *kratos*. Here is translated as "might" and is defined as *demonstrated or visible power* — a power that is *eruptive* and *tangible*. Thus, this is not hypothetical power but real power that is irresistible and overpowering. Basically, Paul was praying for all believers to have an encounter with the glory of God because he knew from personal experience that it will release explosive, superhuman power that produces extraordinary, unparalleled results that can be tangibly experienced.

How is this dynamic power released? Paul said it's "by God's Spirit" (Ephesians 3:16). The word "by" is the Greek word *dia*, which means *by* or *through* and indicates *agency* and *instrumentality*. The word *dia* also carries the idea of *going back and forth again and again in order to go all the way through*, as one who crosses to the other side. Here, we find the never-give-up work of the Spirit to produce the power of God in us.

Where does this empowerment of the Spirit take place? Paul said, "in the inner man" (Ephesians 3:16). The word "in" here is the Greek word *eis*, which means *into* and indicates the location this work is taking place and that it's *ongoing* and *progressive*. The word "inner" is the Greek word *eso*, and indicates *inner, interior,* or *inside*. Altogether, this verse informs us that the longer we walk with the Lord, the more powerful we become in our inner man every time we encounter the Lord.

To Welcome Christ As a Permanent Resident

In Ephesians 3:17, Paul's prayer for believers continues. Here, he prays, "That Christ may dwell in your hearts by faith; that ye, being rooted and grounded in love." The word "dwell" here is the Greek word *katoikeo*, a compound of *kata* and *oikeo*. The preposition *kata* means *down*, and the word *oikeo* means *I dwell, I live*, or *I reside*. When compounded, the word *katoikeo* depicts *settling down and being established in a new home and making oneself feel comfortable there*. This word is also used to describe *a permanent resident*.

It is Paul's deep desire that Jesus settle down and become a permanent resident "in your heart." The word "in" is the Greek word *en*, which identifies the place where Christ lives by His Spirit. And the word "hearts" is *kardias*, from the Greek word *kardia*, describing *the human heart*. Thus, it is the central organ that pumps blood into all the body. Here again, Paul points to our inner man or core as the place where Christ settles down and makes Himself at home. He is not a temporary guest that comes and goes; He is to be a permanent resident.

Paul says this indwelling of the Spirit is experienced "by faith." Once more we see the Greek word *dia* translated here as "by," meaning *by* or *through*, and it indicates *agency* and *instrumentality*. This word tells us that Jesus dwells in our hearts *through the instrumentality* or *agency* of faith. The purpose for Christ taking up residence in our hearts is that we may be "…rooted and grounded in love" (Ephesians 3:17).

The Greek sentence structure here reverses the order to read, "…That in love you may be rooted and grounded." The emphasis is on "love," which is the Greek word *agape*, denoting the unconditional, indescribable love of God. That is what He wants you to be rooted and grounded in — His love.

In Greek, the word "rooted" is *rhidzoo*, and it means *deeply rooted*, like *a plant with deep roots*. Expanding this imagery is the word "grounded" — the Greek word *themelioo*, which means *to be established, like a solid, strong foundation upon which a mighty structure can be built*. When you're rooted and grounded deeply in God's indescribable love, your roots have a foundation you can really build your life upon.

To Fully Comprehend Christ's Love

To this, Paul prayed, "May [you] be able to comprehend with all saints what is the breadth, and length, and depth, and height; And to know the love of Christ…" (Ephesians 3:18,19). Interestingly, the word "may" at the beginning of verse 18 is again the Greek word *hina*, which points to *an express purpose*. In this case, Paul is expressly praying for believers to "…be able to comprehend…the love of Christ…" (Ephesians 3:18,19).

The word "able" in Greek is *exischuo*, a compound of *ek* and *ischuo*. The preposition *ek* means *out*, and *ischuo* pictures *strength* and is derived from *ischuos*, which depicts *a strong man* or *a man with great muscular capabilities*. In this verse, it pictures *the strength deposited in the inner man of believers*. Paul is literally praying that we would be able to comprehend and draw out or extract from Christ's indwelling might.

The phrase "to comprehend" is a translation of the Greek word *katalambano*, which means *to seize*; *to grab hold of*; *to pull down*; *to tackle*; *to conquer*; *to master*; or *to hold under one's power*. Basically, Paul was praying that the believers — which includes us — would be able to seize, tackle, conquer, and master the love of God "with all the saints." The word "with" here is the Greek word *sun*, and it means *in partnership*, which is something that should be equally experienced by all saints.

Again, Paul prayed that we "may be able to comprehend with all saints *what is* the breadth, and length, and depth, and height; And to know the love of Christ…" (Ephesians 3:18,19). We see the phrase "what is" — the Greek word *ti*, which points to *the most minute detail*; *down-to-the-smallest-detail type of knowledge*. The use of this word means that God wants to give a revelation beyond general information. Specifically, He wants to give you a very concrete understanding of the *breadth*, *length*, *depth*, and *height* of His love. Look at the meaning of each of these dimensions:

- "Breadth" — the Greek word *platos*, meaning *breadth* and is used to describe *the farthest ends of the earth*, hence, *the farthest expanse*.

- "Length" — the Greek word *mekos*, meaning *length* and is used to depict *greatness*.

- "Depth" — the Greek word *bathos*, meaning *the deepest parts of the sea* and can denote *deep thoughts*, *deep spiritual truths*, or *deeply laid plans*.

- "Height" — the Greek word *hupsos*, meaning *height* and pictures *what is elevated*; it denotes *eminence*.

So, the more you grasp the breadth, length, depth, and height of Christ's love, the more you understand the farthest expanse, the greatness, the elevated position, and the eminence of who Christ is and the deep spiritual truths and deeply laid plans He has for you.

To Be Filled With All the Fullness of God

In Ephesians 3:19, Paul reiterates the vital importance of knowing and understanding the love of Christ. He prayed that we would come "…to know the love of Christ, which passeth knowledge, that ye might be filled with all the fulness of God." The word "know" here is *gnonai*, from *ginosko*, which means *I know, I perceive, I realize*, or *I recognize*, and it carries the idea of *knowing by experience*. The word "love" is the Greek word *agape*, which describes *Christ's divine love*. These words clearly tell us that God doesn't want us to just have a head knowledge of His love. Rather, He longs for us to have an ever-expanding personal experience of His love.

Notice that Paul tells us Christ's love "passeth knowledge." The word "passeth" is a translation of the Greek word *huperballo*, a compound of the words *huper* and *ballo*. The preposition *huper* describes *something that is above and beyond what is normal* or *something that is exceeding or surpassing*, and the word *ballo* means *to hurl or to throw*. When compounded to form the word *huperballo*, it pictures something like an archer who aims his arrow at the target but shoots way over the top of it. Hence, it depicts *something beyond the range of anything considered normal* or *something that is unparalleled*.

The use of the word *huperballo* here indicates that God wants you to really know and comprehend the love of Christ. Along with studying and getting as much understanding and mental knowledge as you can, God wants to give you an experience with Christ's unparalleled *agape* love that far surpasses mere knowledge.

That is why Paul prayed, "…That ye might be filled with all the fulness of God" (Ephesians 3:19). Here again, we see the word "that" — the Greek word *hina* — which points to *an express purpose* — that you "might be filled." This phrase is a translation of the Greek word *plerothete*. It is from *pleroo*, which means *to be completely filled; to fill completely*; or *filled to the point of overflowing or the point of satisfaction*. The use of this word tells us

God's intention is not just to touch your spirit, but to completely fill your spirit to the point of overflowing. In fact, He desires to fill you "with all the fullness of God."

The word "with" is the Greek word *eis*, which means *into* and indicates this work is *ongoing* and *progressive*. The word "all" in Greek is *pan*, and it means *all* or *all-inclusive, leaving nothing out*. Lastly is the word "fulness" — the Greek word *pleroma* — which means *the sum total, fullness*, or *superabundance* of God. That's how much fullness of the Spirit God wants to give to you!

Pulling Together Both of Paul's Prayers

When we look at all these verses in Ephesians 1:15-19 and in Ephesians 3:14-19, we find that God, the Father of glory, wants to give us a personal encounter with Himself. Through our experience, He will replicate His glory and impart, supply, and furnish us with a spirit of wisdom (special insight) — even revelation. He will pull back the veil so that we can see and understand what we've never seen and understood before. Likewise, He will empower us with the might of His Spirit and enable us to understand and experience with all believers the breadth, length, height, and depth of Christ's love.

Have you been touched by the love of God? Have you experienced His power? That's wonderful. But there's more! You have more space in you, and God wants you to be filled with all the fullness of Himself! He wants to fill you, your family, your friends, and your entire church!

STUDY QUESTIONS

> **Study to shew thyself approved unto God, a workman that needeth not to be ashamed, rightly dividing the word of truth.**
> **— 2 Timothy 2:15**

1. What is one of the greatest takeaways from this study that you really want to remember?
2. Take a few minutes to carefully read over Ephesians 3:14-20 and Ephesians 1:15-19. How would you say these passages on divine revelation are *similar*? How are they uniquely *different*?
3. Part of Paul's prayer in Ephesians 3 is for us to be rooted and grounded in God's love So what do you know about God's love? If

there is any subject you need to "major" in, God's love is at the top of the list! Revisit these important basics on the love of God.

- How do you receive God's love? (*See* Romans 5:5.)
- How did God prove His love to you once and for all? (*See* Romans 5:8; and First John 3:16; 4:9,10.)
- What did God's great love for you move Him to do? (*See* John 3:16; and Ephesians 2:4-9.)
- Out of His great love, what has He made you? (*See* First John 3:1,2; and Romans 8:15.)
- What does a deep revelation of God's love evict from your life? (*See* First John 4:18.)
- How does the love of God grow in you? (*See* First John 4:7-17.)

PRACTICAL APPLICATION

> But be ye doers of the word, and not hearers only, deceiving your own selves.
> —James 1:22

1. Your *heart* — the core of who you are — is where Christ wants to settle down and live. His Spirit doesn't want to be a guest that comes and goes; He wants to be a permanent resident. Be honest: Do you think Jesus feels welcome and at home in your heart? Do you treat Him as a guest who occasionally visits or as a permanent resident in your life? If He were standing visibly in front of you right now, what do you think He would say He loves about living in you? What do you think He would be grieved over and desire that you would change?
2. Along with having a deep revelation of Christ's love, God wants you to be filled with the *fullness of Him* (*see* Ephesians 3:19). Carefully meditate on these scriptures concerning the fullness of God, and jot down what the Holy Spirit reveals to you.

> **For in Him {Jesus} the whole fullness of Deity (the Godhead) continues to dwell in bodily form [giving complete expression of the divine nature]. And you are in Him, made full and having come to fullness of life [in Christ you too are filled with the Godhead — Father, Son and Holy Spirit — and reach full**

> spiritual stature]. And He is the Head of all rule and authority [of every angelic principality and power].
>
> (Colossians 2:9,10 *AMPC*)

> For out of His fullness (abundance) we have all received [all had a share and we were all supplied with] one grace after another and spiritual blessing upon spiritual blessing and even favor upon favor and gift [heaped] upon gift.
>
> (John 1:16 *AMPC*)

3. Friend, God wants to give a revelation beyond general information about His great love for you. Take time now to pray: *Father, I pray just as the apostle Paul prayed — that You would give me and my family a deep, ever-expanding revelation of Your immeasurable love. Let us experience and understand the breadth, length, height, and depth of it! I pray for a fresh encounter with Your glory and an impartation of a spirit of wisdom and revelation. May all of us be strengthened by Your Spirit in the inner man and be filled with all the fullness of You. In Jesus' Name. Amen!*

Notes

Notes

Notes

CLAIM YOUR FREE RESOURCE!

As a way of introducing you further to the teaching ministry of Rick Renner, we would like to send you free of charge his teaching CD, "How To Receive a Miraculous Touch From God."

In His earthly ministry, Jesus commonly healed *all* who were sick of *all* their diseases. In this profound message, learn about the manifold dimensions of Christ's wisdom, goodness, power, and love toward all humanity who came to Him in faith with their needs.

☑ YES, I want to receive Rick Renner's monthly teaching letter!

Simply scan the QR code to claim this resource or go to:
renner.org/claim-your-free-offer

WITH US!

renner.org

- facebook.com/rickrenner • facebook.com/rennerdenise
- youtube.com/rennerministries • youtube.com/deniserenner
- instagram.com/rickrrenner • instagram.com/rennerministries_
  instagram.com/rennerdenise

www.ingramcontent.com/pod-product-compliance
Lightning Source LLC
Chambersburg PA
CBHW061255040426
42444CB00010B/2385